WITHDRAWN

Books by Kay Boyle

Novels

GENERATION WITHOUT FAREWELL

THE SEAGULL ON THE STEP

HIS HUMAN MAJESTY

"1939"

A FRENCHMAN MUST DIE

AVALANCHE

PRIMER FOR COMBAT

MONDAY NIGHT

DEATH OF A MAN

MY NEXT BRIDE

GENTLEMEN, I ADDRESS YOU
   PRIVATELY

YEAR BEFORE LAST

PLAGUED BY THE NIGHTINGALE

Stories and Novelettes

NOTHING EVER BREAKS EXCEPT
   THE HEART

THREE SHORT NOVELS

THE SMOKING MOUNTAIN

THE CRAZY HUNTER

THE WHITE HORSES OF VIENNA

THE FIRST LOVER

WEDDING DAY

THIRTY STORIES

Poetry

TESTAMENT FOR MY STUDENTS

COLLECTED POEMS

A GLAD DAY

AMERICAN CITIZEN

For Children

THE YOUNGEST CAMEL

PINKY, THE CAT WHO LIKED TO
   SLEEP

PINKY IN PERSIA

Memoirs

THE AUTOBIOGRAPHY OF
   EMANUEL CARNEVALI
Compiled and Edited
   by Kay Boyle

BEING GENIUSES TOGETHER
Revised and Supplemented
   by Kay Boyle

Testament for my students

ST. PAUL PUBLIC LIBRARY

KAY BOYLE

Testament for

PS
3503
.O9357
T4

A15837

ST. PAUL PUBLIC LIBRARY

my students

and other poems

1970

DOUBLEDAY & COMPANY, INC.

GARDEN CITY, NEW YORK

Poems in this book have appeared in the following publications: *Testament for My Students, Thunderstorm in South Dakota, A Short Poem in Color, A Square Dance For a Square, A Poem For Arthur,* first appeared in *The Southern Review; For James Schevill, On the Occasion of His Arrest,* Copyright © 1969 by The Huntsville Library Association; *For Marianne Moore's Birthday, November 15, 1967* and *A Poem in One Sentence, Twigs IV,* Copyright © 1968 by Bruce Bennett Brown, Editor *Twigs* magazine, Pikeville College Press, Pikeville College, Pikeville, Kentucky; *World Tour, A Poem About Black Power, The Lost Dogs of Phnom Penh* reprinted from February 1965, January 1967, March 1967 issues of *Liberation,* Copyright © 1965, 1967 by *Liberation; A Poem About Jews,* first published in The Harvard Advocate, Centennial Issue; *A Valentine For Harry Crosby,* Dedicated to Robert McAlmon, *A Letter to Francis Picabia, In Defense of Homosexuality, Glad Day* by Kay Boyle, published by New Directions; *A Poem of Love, Love;* Dedicated to Terre Des Hommes, The Catholic Worker; some other poems appeared in *Collected Poems* by Kay Boyle, published by Alfred A. Knopf, Inc., of which *A Poem of Gratitude for Caresse Crosby* first appeared in *Poetry, The New Emigration* in *The Nation, A Communication to Nancy Cunard* in *New Republic.*

Library of Congress Catalog Card Number 76-100494
Copyright © 1938, 1956, 1959, 1962,
1965, 1967, 1968, 1970 by Kay Boyle
All Rights Reserved
Printed in the United States of America
First Edition

THIS BOOK IS DEDICATED TO SONIA SANCHEZ

Contents

Testament for my students

Testament for my students, 1968-1969

Each year you came jogging or loping down that hall
Bearded or not, sweet emissaries from Arizona
Montana, Illinois, Mass., beneath the light silk hair
Or the dark, or the natural crown, skulls crushable, ribs breakable
This year and last wearing sandals in order to run fast
At your temples pools of blood always trembled
And I would see them spill.

Lodged in the red partitions of your hearts
(Where your fathers reigned for a brief time)
On the palpitating thrones of auricle left or ventricle right
Legs crossed, fluently at ease, sat such brothers as Baudelaire
Melville, Poe, sometimes Shakespeare, Genet, Rimbaud; or sisters
Like Dickinson, Brontë, Austin, needlepoint set aside for that afternoon
Or Gertrude Stein telling you over and over how Americans were
    doggedly made
Your fingers, even though broken, crazily beckoned
These brothers and sisters and others to you, in your lungs
Enough breath remained to summon them all by name.
These lines are set down for a reason that's suddenly gone out the
    window
For I can recall now only your faces: Woodie Haut, Shawn Wong,
    Rebhun, Turks, Alvarado
And how many more. Or I catch now and then the sound of a voice

From a long way away, saying something like: "Poetry is for the people
And it should represent the people." (You can say that again, Woodie)
Or saying: "If the academic poets want to keep poetry for themselves,
    then
They're no different from the administration of this college
Which wants to keep education for the select few. I am inclined
To agree with Eldridge Cleaver and the BSU that you are part of the
    problem
Or else you are part of the solution." Or maybe Alvarado's voice can
    be heard
Barely whispering under the campus trees: "Don't make too much noise
You might wake up the middle class."

Once I read in a book that the ear of the Oriental records sound so
    swiftly
So sharply, that the falling of a rose petal from a vase will rouse him
From his sleep. That spring, Shawn Wong awoke to see the mounted
    police charge, yet
It was "the small white flowers trampled in the grass, and the blood
Of poets lying near the broken stems" that stirred his gentle dreams
Or Rebhun will flip aside the armor of arrogance he wears to type on
    the required paper
"If you wish to see mankind, look into the glass. If you look long enough
One man will become ten men, and then a hundred men, and then a
    thousand
We saw the police striking out in a sadly strange fury. Each time
The baton fell on bone, the pain was felt by all of us. For
Behind the physical manifestations of our fervor we are one man
Asking for another world, a world in which we are less tools
Of an impersonal power, and ten or a hundred or a thousand men of
    flesh and blood."

THE UNGARBLED STORY THAT UNFOLDED BEFORE ME

Well, the incident I want to tell you about came to pass in a college
small enough to put in your pocket. In the northern sticks of California

14

it was, where a middle-aged white professor got up on the auditorium stage to introduce a black psychiatrist to what was left of a student body scattered in the seats on a rainy afternoon. The two principal characters had beards, but no two beards could have been more different one from the other. The black man's was a handsome addition to his face. The professor's was thin and ailing, but still he had managed to train it to do his bidding. Whenever he turned his shrunken head, the point of his beard jerked accusingly in still another direction, indicating with severity that education lay, if you were only able to see it, in that dusty corner right over there.

"Dr. Parnassus is not just a psychiatrist who is black," the professor began this memorable introduction. "He is a *black* psychiatrist. I hope you can all grasp that distinction." For some reason nobody in the audience said: "Right on, brother" as he stood looking out over the auditorium, his beard pointing this way and then that. The black psychiatrist himself had instantly become expendable as he sat on the stage fingering his yellow silky tie. "There are not many around," continued the professor, and this was certainly the truest thing that had been said that afternoon, for the psychiatrist was the only black face within a mile or two.

And then the professor turned to the exciting subject of himself. For a number of years, he said, he had been interested in the problems of minority groups, and in particular in the black man in the black ghetto. ("I say, that's awfully good of you, old crutch," said somebody out of the top drawer of my English mementos.) And now the professor charmed everyone there with the avowal that he was about to lay the foundation for, or to initiate, or else to inaugurate, a course at this up and coming institution for the study of a Black Studies Program, and his beard waved sparsely in the direction of the psychiatrist. "I hope to have many eminent black scholars come to talk here on the subject of a study for the development of what may eventually become, we hope," he said.

"Those who have been closely involved in educational procedures," the professor proceeded, excluding the audience from that happy experience, "have established beyond question that there is no possibility of successfully inaugurating—or initiating, if you prefer—or, indeed, laying the foundations for, any course unless that inauguration or initiation has been preceded by a long term study in depth of what it may be advisable to undertake at some future time." There was a perceptible movement of restlessness among the seated, including the psychiatrist, and the professor's beard jerked toward the door marked "Exit," but no one rose to go. It could have been that no one in the history of the college had ever got up and walked out in distaste for what was being said.

The students in this place wore marvelously clean tan Levis, and navy blue windbreakers. The young men's hair was splendidly trimmed, and the girls' hair was anything but long and untamed. They all had regular shoes on their feet. It was another era entirely, and the things the professor was saying kept carrying us even farther back on the assembly line of his eager self-esteem. "This is somewhat of a pilot course I am initiating," were his words. "I might say it took a good deal of personal ingenuity to get it started, for it has a touch of revolutionary daring about it." (Oh, how dreary, dreary, can the purveyors of education be if you let them get out of hand for even two minutes, and this is what had taken place. That's what rock and roll is for; I knew it with sweet exhilaration then. It's the only thing loud enough to drown out the voices of the cautious of our day.) "A pre-study of a Black Studies Program could scarcely be considered anarchistic in concept," the professor hastened to add, his beard ready to do battle for him if it came to that. "Wisdom and reason are not the most popular words in our current vocabulary, but I still find them useful. This semester will be devoted to studying with patience and wisdom what reasonable procedure we can develop which will lead . . ."

There are times when there is nothing left to do but take a decision, and now that moment had come. It would have been taken even had the psychiatrist, after glancing at his wristwatch, not risen to the occasion and made one step in the direction of the lectern. The professor turned his head in irritation, and the words died in his mouth. His beard pointed directly to the chair that the psychiatrist had vacated, but the black man had no intention of sitting down again. He tapped the

16

crystal of his watch with his long forefinger. "I have a plane to catch
in about three-quarters of an hour. I have to get back to Watts," he said,
and so he was allowed to laugh out loud.

Each year their eyes, midwestern gray or cattle-range blue
Or jet like the ghetto, held visions of what might be achieved
They wrote of the river bank that colonized men slide down
In Fanon's prose, to cleanse themselves of the violence of the dance
Or wrote: "We all sense the pressure of black passion
We lose balance in the presence of the black man's frenzied
Momentum toward autonomy. The urgent tempo with which
He hurls himself at life dazzles us." When I see Victor Turks
Again I'll ask him if he was listening when Sartre spoke
For the dead Fanon, saying that all the inexcusable, the uncondonable
     acts
Of violence on the part of those at bay are neither sound nor fury
Nor the resurrection of savage instincts, but are part of
The anguished process of man as he re-creates his lost identity
"We should accept the black man's advances toward self-possession,"
     Victor kept writing
Looking up for a moment from *Les Fleurs du Mal, Le Diable au Corps*
"As the means of his salvation. Let *him,* for once, not the white man
Not the European, not Western civilization, but *him* set the example
For us all to follow." It might be in this way, the trembling wind
And the young midwestern voices whistled softly, that we could regain
Our lost humanity. There were many more. There was Father Jim
     Hietter
Muted laughter, muted grief, melodious student, saying to me
That Christian hate had masqueraded for so long as Christian love
The time had come to call it by its rightful name. "Stuff your holiday
     stomachs"
He wrote at Christmas. "Paint your world with colored lights
And sleep   sleep   sleep

There is Police on Earth, and Eichmann carols the countdown
To the Christ child's birth."

There were others, among them Chris Miller who bought ankle-high
    sneakers
With air vents, like portholes, near the soles. He loved them so
That he walked with his dark head lowered to watch the pure white
Canvas keeping pace with his thoughts, his talk. "A self
Which does not transcend itself is dead," he said. I see the sideways
Shy, dark smile and the pointed chin. "So let me rise into life
And die naked like an amimal, which I am," he wrote, "and be buried
In my mother's earthy body, to rot, and to fertilize the soil. Thus
Death will be my final offering to God."

You were not afraid of death, sweet emissaries from Arizona
Montana, Mass., and Illinois; or of mace, or of handcuffs or clubs
And there's one thing more: you bore the terrible knowledge
That colonized men and poets wear their sharpest pain on the surface
Of their flesh, like an open sore
But this year the writers you honored were, with the crack of a baton
Turned suddenly to stone. Their tongues were hacked from their
    throats
By bayonets, and the blows came steadily, savagely, on the exquisite
Brittleness of bone. What good were the poets to you then, Baudelaire,
    Whitman
Rimbaud, Poe? "All the good in the world!" you shouted out
Through the blood in your mouths. They were there beside you on
The campus grass, Shakespeare, Rilke, Brontë, Radiguet
Yeats, Apollinaire, their fingers on the pulse in your wrists
Their young arms cradling your bones.

                                                    (1969)

For James Baldwin

Black cat, sweet brother,
Walk into the room
On cat's feet where I lie dying
And I'll start breathing regularly again.
Witch doctor for the dispossessed,
Saint tipping your halo to the evicted,
The world starts remembering its postponed loyalties
When I call out your name. I knew you hot nights
When you kept stepping
The light fantastic to music only the wretched
Of the earth could hear; blizzards
In New Hampshire when you wore
A foxskin cap, its tail red as autumn
On your shoulder. In the waters of the Sound
You jumped the ripples, knees knocking,
Flesh blue with brine, your fingers
Cold as a dead child's holding mine.

You said it all, everything
A long time ago before anyone else knew
How to say it. This country was about to be
Transformed, you said; not by an act of God,
Nothing like that, but by us,
You and me. Young blacks saw Africa emerging
And knew for the first time, you said,

That they were related to kings and
To princes. It could be seen
In the way they walked, tall as cypresses,
Strong as bridges across the thundering falls.

                             In the question period once
A lady asked isn't integration a two-way
Street, Mr. Baldwin, and you said
You mean you'll go back to Scarsdale tonight
And I'll go back to Harlem, is that the two ways
You mean?

We are a race in ourselves, you and I,
Sweet preacher. I talked with our ancestors
One night in dreams about it
And they bade me wear trappings of gold
And speak of it everywhere; speak of it on
The exultant mountain by day, and at night
On river banks where the stars touch fingers.
They said it might just save the world.

                                        (1969)

The Jews among the nations

FOR ERICH KAHLER

Your sentences cast print and paper to the winds,
Become a crowd so dense there is no parting
Thigh from thigh or man from men, become a tapestry
Of flesh, of human eyes, that fire must shrink from,
Cower before. Your hastening voice describes a temple stone
By stone, a solid residence in which
A tribe, a proverb, an astonishment, may dwell.

Time you define as a long march obscured
By shouting. But time is like a desert where
Your quick acuity dispels the veils of mirage so that one can see
There could have been no trees, no water for the bending reeds,
No reeds, only the semblance of these, and the loose sand
Slipping beneath the vagrant foot of man. You say
That those who drown—whether in water or sand or in their own
    despair—
Are not effaced, but live in the tribal might of "an invisible
Mysterious deity," changeless and burning, like the pitiless, golden
Gazing of the sun. Those who survive, you say, live singularly apart,
    elusive
As strangers among other men.

You quote the Babylonian Talmud saying
Of the Jews: "This people has been likened
To the dust, it has been likened to the stars. Sinking,

It is debased to dust. Rising, it is lifted to the stars."
You note the prophecy that the lives of these men shall
Hang in doubt before them all their days, that they shall be given
Trembling hearts, and sorrow of mind,
That the soles of their feet shall know no rest.
These things amaze me that you say.

Your clarity gives the labyrinths a lantern, crosses
Rivers by means of planets, climbs the arid hills of what remains
To man, hastens, hastens, through the centuries, bidding the Jew,
"Self-critical, self-ironical," to enter by the same door,
Pass under the same arch, as the German "arrested and immured"
In national identity, recalling that Jews alone
Inhabit as fluid men the kingdom of a temple built
Within a long astonishment, live in the wisdom
Of a proverb I had not known was there,
Or anywhere.

(1969)

A poem in one sentence

FOR CLAY PUTMAN

It was more than could have been hoped for
In that lecture hall or theater of the mind crowded
With students in motorcycle dress or else
Bare-legged, feet in sandals, hair amazingly golden,
The boys' longer than the girls'; here, where the tiered
Tilted rows held the restless young (interrupted, as if for comment,
By the weary weary faces of ourselves); it was more
Than could have been expected, your request, tentatively proffered,

That each child cherish a self to which he (or she) might return
When the collective voice had ceased its clamor, that each maintain
A self whose signature did not alter with the season, for
The cheques that history would require that self to put its name to
Would be drawn on another bank (undoubtedly), the currency not
　　the same
(As a certainty); requesting that they recall their individual names
Once the outcry here (or anywhere) had died; and if they could not
Answer you then, I promise you they will a long time after,
When their feet are shod, and their hair shorn, each remembering
And answering the request you made in the convocation hall.

(1968)

23

For James Schevill

ON THE OCCASION OF HIS ARREST

The tongue that serves in courtroom is alien metal,
Having to do with handcuffs, rustproof bars, and interference with
    activity,
With guilt beneath the nearly annihilated sun, or lack of guilt
Beneath the perishable, soft flowering of apple trees.
Anvilled from one side of the mouth, hot words (like outcry,
Protest, disturbance, felony) are cooled. The courtroom tongue
Clangs "bail, suspended sentence, misdemeanor, own recognizance."
Out of my own recognizance I say the language in which I write
This to you has gone underground; waits as the enduring
Passages of history mingle with the roots of trees, with stones,
With hidden streams. In spring's long sweet conniving,
This language that we sense but do not hear has no alternatives to offer,
Does not acknowledge fear.

In courtroom, classroom, the IBM contraptions shudder. The cold
Of their metal clarions "failed the course," "incomplete,"
"Has not fulfilled the requirements," lacking the range to whisper
"Music" to the uproar. They cannot lift the welded helmets from
    their brows
To see trees fall like executed men. "Metal, metal!" they clang in the
    courtroom;

"Metal!" But in the green leaves of a covert season, poets alone are
    summoned
As witnesses. The fingerprints of poets, blue on file cards,
Speak indelibly of the separateness of man.

(*1968*)

For Marianne Moore's birthday

NOVEMBER 15, 1967

I wish you triumphs that are yours already,
And also wish to say whatever I have done
Has been in admiration (imitation even)
Of all you marvelously proliferate. Once someone
Turned to me and said in lowered voice (because you too were in
    the room)
That William Carlos Williams gave to you at sight that
Singular esteem known by no other name save love. These words were
Spoken perhaps a half century ago
(In Monroe Wheeler's Eastside flat) when you
Wore amber braids around your head. And now,
As then, I cannot write this book or that
Without you. You have always been
Nightingale, baseball fan, librarian of my visions,
Poised on a moving ladder in the sun.

(1968)

The lost dogs of Phnom Penh

Do not stab my heart like this, scabby vagrants, garbage hounds, waiting
For the truck to sail on its tide of odor into port.
At one-thirty in the morning (now, as then), truck wheels are
    hushed by the monsoon rains
Or the clamor of the Asian stars, and you are there. You have
No growl in throat, no snarl on lip, you do not shout names at one
    another,
Death, the ineluctable, being so near. You wait on brittle haunches,
    dream
Of the fine enamel of eggshells not quite scraped of their contents; of
A strip of lettuce glistening with the solid gold of oil.

Back in this land of packaged meats, at one-thirty in the morning
    (now, as then),
I think of you, of your ribs curved like the wicker of crickets' cages,
The desiccated crickets of your hearts no longer chirping behind the bars.
I think of you, lost dogs, of the eternal wishbones of your breasts.
Under the streetlights you form a motley alphabet,
Unsuitable for use in any language. When one of you lies down,
He draws the wooden links of a tail around his elbows.
His body shapes a weary "m," humped like a camel, in defeat.
Another of you becomes the letter "u," like a sick lamb curved
    across the shepherd's
Forearm. But nowhere among you can I find a "t," high as a whistle
    keening

Beyond the reach of human ear; nowhere among you is there an "e,"
The beginning of that ironic "enough." I seek these letters
To complete the brief word "mute" that is closed, fleshless,
Bloodless, in the cold anvils of your jaws. At one-thirty in the morning,
The radio in my kitchen tells me that America, my country, is the
    garbage capital of the world.

Lost dogs of Phnom Penh, cry out, cry out, as men cry out
Across the intricate frontier of broken, still unbroken, Vietnam,
Under the same unfaltering stars!

                                                    (*1966*)

A poem of love

The day you told me you had a bank account
Of inestimable proportions, too great
For balancing in any checkbook,
More multitudinous than the loose silver of the Milky Way,
I entered without genuflection the crypt, the bank vault,
Of the forest, trod moss softer than folding money,
At the cashier's window asked for dandelion heads
To hoard for their coarse gold. With this currency
I have acquired a palm tree here, across the fence,
Beyond the Inca daisies which, according to prophecy,
Were transformed to golden rods by the commandment
Of an oracle whose dark voice bade the descendants of the Sun God
To move northward in search of buzzard dollars, double eagles, dough.

Being an entire sunset away, you cannot see this palm tree.
It is luxuriant as a peacock's tail, rainbowed by mist
In the early morning, emerald by starlight. It is not lanky like a giraffe.
Nor is it parched for speech. Hundreds of birds talk in its sixteen storeys.
One day you will race the sun across
America and say: "Why didn't you tell me
About this palm tree that you bought on credit?"
And I will answer: "I told you once when we awoke,
But you have forgotten. Its roots have opened
A savings account in the floating capital of sand that no worm riddles,
Somewhere under the invested asphalt of this marginal soil."

At night,
In the tentative wind, it talks your drowsy lingo,
Its palm feathers whispering of earthquake fluctuations.
I do not know on what stock exchange I bid for it, or
What dividends it should pay, or not pay, annually,
But only that it is gold-edged at sunrise, and that
Its mint par of international exchange is love.

(1966)

Dedicated to *Terre des Hommes*

> Terre des Hommes *is a Swiss organization that attempted to arrange the removal of wounded children from Vietnam to European hospitals.*

Terre des Hommes, consider how strong your voice is.
I can hear it, far as I am from the glaciers where I once lived,
Yodeling out to those who hang on ropes in the blue crevasses
Or dangle from rock, the cord unraveling swiftly, swiftly.
They are lost in a mountainous and eternal country,
The landscape tight-lipped, gigantic, as they swing, grimacing,
Deaf to the high clear yodel saying: This is the way, this is the way!

(I saw the children dancing in Southeast Asia in August,
Dancing daintily, prettily, with their scarves of napalm,
Their cloaks of phosphorus. These expensive gifts we have sent to them
They will be permitted to keep forever. The opal wings
Of the tissue that once was epidermis contrast so
Effectively with their dark and alien skins.)

Terre des Hommes, I hear you calling out that there is time
To return before the last storm whistles down from the north,
Before the ropes unravel to a thread. "In Europe,"
You write on the stubborn snows, in letters as tall
As the palm trees of another continent; "in Europe
We have found several hundred beds." You draw an arrow,

31

Showing where the Swiss lakes lie, where cows wear garlands
Of gentians around their necks, where children
May rest for a while beneath the ether cones.

(In the jungle of their homeland, no silky tiger moves,
No zebra stamps on the plain, no elephant trumpets, no water buffalo
Ruminates, shifting rice paddy greens between his jaws. Leaves
Have died silently under the stutter of helicopter spray,
And the children, dancing without gas masks, turn toward us
And smile at their own deaths, wondering, but not wishing to intrude.)

For a long time your yodeling went unanswered, *Terre des Hommes,*
Then the word came, written on heavy white paper, white
As the White House. "Dear *Terre des Hommes,*" it began,
And it went on saying: "The American Air Force cannot be used to
    transport the children
Of Vietnam who might be in need of medical attention. There exists
No American financial means to assist your activities.
Yours truly." And the signature? I swear it is not mine.
I wouldn't have had the time to write the letter out. I'm working
Creatively, trying out variations on the theme they dance,
These children who glide through the moonlight, bat-colored now,
Screeching like bats. Their dance cannot be mazurka, not polka,
Not bolero, not hornpipe, or jig. It must be
A regional dance to which they step carefully, carefully,
So as not to disturb the flesh that still clings to their bones.

(*1966*)

A poem about Black Power

Let us grow old with modesty,
See with our rheumy, failing eyes
That prophets wear cloaks of fire now
(As then). Let us not pound our canes
On the boards for order as we limp across
The blazing stage we knew must blaze.
"Where, where is the red glow spelling 'Exit'?"
Panic cries out; "where, where the asbestos curtain that must fall
Between us and the footlights of our rage?"
Sweethearts, the script has changed (or perhaps not changed),
And with it the stage directions which advise
Lowered voices, genteel asides,
And the white hand slowly turning the dark page.

Let us grow old admitting we saw the fire, the savage betrayed eyes,
Heard the screaming terror of their deaths, and wrote a letter,
Nicely phrased, to someone else, and slept then,
As the old sleep, nodding, remembering. *Remembering what?*
That four little black girls died in a church?
Are we quite certain that we heard their cries?

When they cite Gandhi to you please recall
That he built fires hot enough and tall
Enough to light the whole of India. I was a child then
And, troubled by their flames, each evening knelt and asked my mother

What he burned. "Clothing and rice," she answered,
"Clothing and rice in time of want and famine. Clothing and rice
England had sent in charity to change the look of history,
And did not change it, for Gandhi turned that bribery to flame."

Those fires consumed the debris of my youth,
Burned steadily, burn still, and now I see the lone immortal bird
That wings up from their ash, so clear, so plain,
That the old tremble and tremble and tremble, and cannot say its name.

(1966)

Thunderstorm in South Dakota

All that blazing day, swift-breasted swallows, envious crows, grackles
    in trees,
Gathered in roadside conference. At dusk
Winged ants splattered the windshield, dying indelibly.
No ripped glove, no kleenex, could efface their gauze
From the glass. At night, on the black pass, the bereft
Sheep slept, and I, bereft, was awakened by fountains of light
Spraying over the granite monuments of clouds, over the towers and
    cornices,
Over this toppling architecture of storm,
And I wrote you:

"I am afraid of the uproar of this demolition,
And reach my hand out in the alien motel bed,
Seeking all that is absent, seeking the pulse
That skips so lightly in your wrist. I remember
The singular wisdom of your hands, their shape,
Their knowledge of many things, the narrow division of your fingers.
It is so different, this thundering of stone, this clamor, this that
    pounds at the window,
Drenching the beasts in their stretches of land on the South Dakota pass;
It is so different from the uncertain pace of your heart, from the far rain,
That is falling, falling, gentle as tears, in Ireland where you are."

(1965)

A short poem in color

Damn it, one shouts, but there is no echo in the forest
For the temper pales with the years; it is no longer
Metal writhing red in the foundry
Of whose impatience, yours or mine?
As one grows old, the hair need not be combed so often
For the wind no longer seizes it
With wild trembling hands.
These things I have read in books,
But I have not been told what season swings
Its searchlight white across the skunk dark of
Philanderings, driving the shadows—black cattle in panic—
Down back ways where men (say men who have refused the midday
Illumination of fidelity) relieve themselves against promiscuous stone
Despite God's admonition scrawled across the granite wall:
"*Mes pauvres enfants, défense d'uriner.*"

(1965)

A poem about the Jews

I have had enough of them, more than enough;
Enough of the pages allotted to them, the margins
Crowded with faces, not as high ground is thronged
With sheep whose lips tear at the parched grass
Between stones, but crowded as subway platforms are
With a mosaic of faces, eloquent beyond lamentation
In the rush hour of returning home.
I have had enough of the silent chapters
Of their history. ("Without outcry"
Is written in every language of their coming and going).
I am sick and tired of every word of it. And you, you haven't
The time to listen, so do not listen. There is so much else to do.

> After some centuries had passed
> The descendants of Abraham
> Took on the bright density of tribes,
> Related not only by common worship
> But by common ancestry. (So they began).
> Crop failures and droughts—the skeleton
> Hand of the parched wind sifting the dust—
> Impelled them to ask, as other nomads had asked,
> Leave to pasture their flocks in the western fringes
> Of the Nile's tidal mouth.
> There, on slopes cropped by the square teeth of
> Sheep, goats, occasional donkeys,

Following highways of emerald bulrushes,
Water to their anklebones, bearded,
These shepherds roamed. They sojourned
A long while in Egypt, speaking their own tongue,
Compliant, peaceful as saints, and were
In acknowledgment reduced to servitude.
(Such was their lot). They who had been freemen,
Their spirits illuminated by loneliness,
Became bondsmen, groaning under
The taskwork of fashioning bricks
From the gold mud slipping under foot,
Bemoaned their destiny as they built Pithom and Ramses,
East of Goshen (cities without subways to herd them
Or housing projects to take them in), crying out
In longing for those places where the name Israel
Lived still, was still whispered on the dunes,
However far.

You have heard all this before.
You know that on one occasion a shepherd wandered
Deeper into the wilderness seeking fresher valleys, and passed
Close by the mountain of Horeb, of Sinai; and there beheld a bush
    alight.
But neither the branches of that bush nor the frail white flowers
Were devoured by the flame. However fiercely they burned,
They did not burn. The shepherd, a little slow of tongue,
Slow of thought even, it is rumored, could find
No explanation for this miracle (in the presence of which
The flocks stood ruminating) until a clear voice spoke in the rush hour
Of the return. The God of the fathers called out from the fire.
It was twilight. There were no stars yet
To bear witness, no clouds to veil the planets had they appeared.
The evening was blue as sapphire, translucent as amethyst.
There was silence
Except for the voice that spoke. It bade
The shepherd lead his people into freedom.

You know how the exodus took place in the petalled springtime
Of the year one thousand two hundred and twenty
Before Christ's name was known.

       And then, to go on with it, in 1093, Peter the Hermit,
       A native of Picardy, set forth on pilgrimage to Jerusalem,
       And in wrath at the miseries of the pilgrims
       Returned to Europe, crying out that the duty of the Church
       Was the deliverance of the holy places from the infidel.
       In Mayence, the Crusaders passed, and the Jews had trouble.
       "The blood of the men mingled with the blood of their wives,"
       It is written, "and the strong, sad blood of the fathers
       Mingled with their children's blood;
       The blood of the brothers with their sisters', the
       Blood of the teachers with their disciples', the
       Blood of the grooms with their brides', the
       Blood of the judges with their scribes', the
       Blood of the infants with their mothers'."
       (We know all this, the wailing, the bemoaning,
       Centuries without end).
       But one thing more, just one,
       And then I'll keep quiet about it.
       In July 1099, the knights in tunics
       Of chain and coats of mail, and the riffraff
       That accompanied them, captured Jerusalem.
       Godfrey of Boulogne was made king; and thus
       Was founded the Latin kingdom of Jerusalem
       Whose life, it is recorded, "was one of the most painful
       Ever penned; a history of almost unredeemed envy,
       Malice, shame; a kingdom that in eighty-eight years
       Would disappear as suddenly as it had come, leaving no trace
       Save the ruins of castles and churches,
       And the countless dead; save a few place names
       And a deathless legacy: the hatred of Christianity
       In the hearts and the marrow of the natives there."

But let me keep history straight.
"The ears of him who hears these things will tingle,
For who has ever heard anything like this?" wrote Solomon bar Samson
Early in his century, asking the question much too soon;
For presently Edessa fell to the Mohammedans, and Pope Eugenius,
Poor man, beside himself, out of his wits, doing his utmost,
Issued a call for a new Crusade. In response to the fiery eloquence
Of St. Bernard, multitudes gathered about the King of France,
About the German Emperor, and again the Jews stretched out their
    necks.
(That is the ancient phrase for it). They thrust forth
Their necks and let the bright knife find its place.
The Germans were not alone in their fury. There were always
The others. There were the virtuous, happy, just, ecclesiastical men,
The pompous, the titled, the revered, of France, England, Spain, all
Those who trembled at the look of features different from their own.
The Germans were not alone—except as each man's judgment of himself
Is secret and isolate, and has no nation's name. The bishops, delicate
    of thought,
Acute of sensibility, sought to protect the outcasts. St. Bernard himself
Permitted no excesses. Christian usurers, he argued, were no better
Than Jewish usurers. (That was gracious of him). But still Jews,
He made clear, should remit interest due from such of those
Who took the Cross.

        At this moment in the wearisome history,
        In the furtive annals on which no light of day, but only
        Gaslight flickers, the instigator was the monk Radulph,
        A pious man, gentle with birds, who in his devotion
        Skipped in monk's attire along the Rhine,
        Preaching that Jews living in the cities and villages
        Should be effaced; like vermin, he specified,
        Like rats; for were not their eyes as avid,
        Their noses twice as long? His teachings
        Bore fruit, and among the hundreds who were quickly slain

(Or who took their children's lives and then their own) was
    Simeon,
The Saint of Treves, returning on foot from England,
    making his way
Along the high road, where, not far from Cologne,
In the Queen Anne's Lace and the dust,
He was done to death by the passing noblemen of that Crusade.

(Young men and young women shall not dance together,
Wrote Judah, the mystic from Italy, the Jewish saint,
But each sex shall dance by itself. No Jew, so his
Teachings went, shall disguise himself in the garments
Of a Christian cleric to escape persecution, or shall
He sew a cross upon his cloak). I can hear you sighing.
I too have no patience left for the regulations of history:
"Jews to move freely, and carry their wares from
Place to place, but not to settle; Jews to hold no
Public offices, inasmuch as they have been
Condemned in expiation to perpetual slavery; Jews
To wear a special dress, or a distinctive sign,
A badge to be pinned or embroidered on their
Garments, a star, yellow in color, over the perfidious heart."
All this happened a long time ago. It's closed
In the pages of books "without outcry." Even the
Equalities they attained are like far, alien music,
Scarcely played: "No toll to be levied on
A Jewish corpse when removed from one city to another, from
One province to another." Cannot the burden finally be laid down?

No, not quite yet, not quite yet. Something has happened.
It is much later. It is July 1964. There are two hundred sailors,
Maybe three hundred, wooden clubs in their hands to fight off
    rattlesnakes,
Water moccasins. They move through the suck of the Mississippi
    swamplands,
Wearing hip boots as they comb the bayous. They drag the Pearl River

(Which yields other bodies, dismembered, bloated, but not those of the
  two Jews
And the Catholic who had left no sign). The frogs and the varmints
  hush their throbbing
As the skiffs paddle in, the orchestra moaning again once
The searchers have passed. It is said that one of the three died
Because of the beard he wore and the shape of his features. It is said
The state ordered coats of armor buckled on to meet the invasion of
  "Jews and other scum."
It is said that Choctaw Indians saw the mob gathering; but Indians
Have been sent back through time to the beginning. They no longer
  have a tongue.
The air was heavy with magnolia, light with the smell of
  honeysuckle.
The land for miles around was silent. The night they lay warm in the
  southern earth,
The bush did not burn. There was no miracle. Yet their names were
  spoken,
Jewish names, shepherds like the other, Goodman and Schwerner,
And one who was Catholic, Chaney; their faces eloquent
Beyond lamentation in the rush hour of returning. Can we say
Now we have heard enough? Can we say the history is done?

(*1965*)

42

A poem for Arthur

You shook the liquid amber tree
And all my earrings fell
From it. Letters had come
From everyone, from
Taxi drivers, homing pigeons, B. J. Chute,
And other members of the National Institute.
My acute despair about one earring
Extinguished the candles of Marianne's birthday cake.
"The earring's lost, the dinner's off!" she cried,
And the Academy elevators rose and fell.
(She sent me a ten-dollar bill to buy another—
Earring, not dinner. She spoke
With delicacy of the eucalyptus leaves,
Emerald and dark on my white dress). But nothing
Came of it until you shook the liquid amber
Tree outside the door, and the pods fell,
Raining their seeds into your scarlet beard,
Into your hair; and I believed then
That earrings have a season, that if you stood
A long time in the rain
There would be earrings, white as hawthorn,

Lying as in Tiffany's on the mauve satin
Of the afternoon. I believed
The candles on the birthday cake would spring to flame
Again, a finger of icing tracing "Marianne—
Marianne Moore," the thirteen letters of her name.

(*1965*)

A square dance for a square

This time the accordions will cry out—not me, for I'll start laughing.
Now that I've learned the Left Square Through,
The Texas Star, the Dip'n Dive, I'm armed with you. I
Won't trip on my three-tiered skirt, but Half Sashay
And Back Track with an Inside Out, an Outside In. I'll
Box the Flea, Shoot That Star, do a Courtesy Turn toward
Where you are. I will not fall and crack my skull, neither
My jaw nor my buckling knee.

To square dance is to stomp, to clap, to yodel out
One's terror. It is a segregated rite, the
Opposite number of the minstrel show. And you, sweet partner
Of men's furtive nights, you Do Sa Do, shuffling but law-abiding,
Warily do the Wrong Way Thar and Cross Trail Through.

    And then
            and then

The intermission comes, returning you
To the pitch and howl of long back alleys
Where the cool cats stray. Above the roofs, past
Known identity, the far stars tremble at their own imaginings,
The shook blood draws a likeness that you
Rip in two. You bring me Hawaiian Sunlight in a paper cup,
Sickened with vitamins, and turn away, taking your fingers

With you. "Hey," I say, "hey, hey! Shuffle
A little longer!" But silence is the numb blue baby
Clutched against your stamping breast. You walk
The parquet flooring of your life with it, stick
A cigar between its gums, throttle it on lighter fluid,
Whisper to it: "Hush, hush, God damn you." But it can't stop.
It's silence already. Who can shut his trap on silence anyway?

There is a curtain that divides your life. The members
Of the cast who have no lines to say
Clamor behind its folds, grimace, and point; and you before it,
Blinded by footlights, uneasily play
The Eight Chain Thru. I cannot
See from where I am, cannot applaud. My hands
Are tied, finger to finger, like a nun's
In prayer. Not upright in the aisle, and not in loge,
Not hunched in gallery, I watch you cross the boards
With lowered head, the shoulders stooped
To guard the heart from onslaught, the body hollowed
Like a palm to hold the measure of outrage you claim.

                                        Shuffler,
They are not yours, the griefs, deaths, losses, burials of
Other men. Neither the See Saw nor the Wagon Wheel describes
Your gait, but something else, something like seeing you walk
A road made luminous by moon at night, each ankle
Dragging with it ball and chain.

            And then
                and then

Your anger stops the music suddenly, rips the accordion in two, snaps
The catgut of fiddle, extracts the piano's teeth from wooden gums
Without a cry. "The dancing has stopped," I say.
"The square dance is finished," I whisper as you walk away.

46

You slept once in a field, close by the lake, and there
In sleep you spoke their names. They came, crowding the grass,
Tougher than daisies, than thistles, than Queen Anne's Lace, until
There was no space for breath. And I that day was every face
That turned toward you: I, the child-hustler from 42nd Street,
Trying the skeleton key in your apartment door, asking to enter
The back bedroom of your despair; I, the illicit roomer with
Briefcase and lowered girlish lids who once, in sleep, had kissed
You on the mouth; and I, the Negro mounting the stairs
Two at a time, for fear, for fear; and I, Brother Infidelious
With glossy hair, pacing the cloistered vineyards of your diocese,
Telling my beads, a girl's high heels beneath
The cassock's hem. Mine were the heels, and mine
The voice that murmured at times in blasphemy, at times in prayer.
I was that workman in the Philadelphia bar, the place dark as a mine
Though it was noon, the underground explosion, the catastrophe
Within the heart or pit already taken place. At the bleak shaft
The women and the unborn children stood, and I was every wife and
     every
Toothless, bereft hag, and every child who cried your name. While you
Black-masked and mute, asked nothing except of one man, skinny and
     quick
As a mosquito, seated at the bar, with legs drawn up to strike the venom
     in;
And I, without the flicker of an eyelash, became him.

But there was the leaping of great rabbits once
In the summer, the splashing of lake fish in the sun.
There was the square dance of tombstones
On needles of frost one November. But never again, never again.
You laughed out loud at the calls: "Allemande Left
Your corner, partner right. Those in the center retain the Star
But release the hands of those outside, then four couples right
And now Left Through, Dixie Grand, and a
Do Paso, Frontier Whirl, and Catch All Eight. Couple Wheel Around

And Weave That Ring, Weave Around, don't touch a thing. Four
    Couples
Susie-Q, bow to your partner, your corner, too,
Wave to the girl across from you." The caller says: "You're doing fine!"
As I crack my skull, my jaw, my knee, when you take
Your hand away from mine.

(1963)

The evening grass

They have an innocence the words
                              Take your own life
Or *took his life*
As if they spoke of your or his accumulated days
Taken in casual accounting walking through
The evening grass no graver not so grave as if
Either you or he had turned and taken
An indifferent woman in the evening grass
                                        But life does not

Go out this quietly not whispering not
Murmuring through the grass but
Differently so differently
                    You heard
The blast his dying made
Know it was not for him alone you wept
And not for him the endless pounding
Of the flagstones with a mallet's wood until
The skull of all men broke that
Dusk until the splintering was your brain's
Glass and his memory's crockery
                              You ran
The jagged staircase of your grief for all
Who say tonight
            tonight
                tonight

Yes LIFE tonight to liquid ears and no
One hears it was for paintings out of frames that
Lean on warehouse walls for all
The lost engravings of the heart wild
Cardiographs of lust you wept for flesh
That had not lingered in his bed for mouths
That did not lie upon his mouth
                              The tide of brine
From eyes and nose roared through the
Seaweed of the evening grass star flowers stayed
While pounding pounding with one hand you flung
The wooden arms of trees upon
The flame their brittle fingers snapping
As they burned Christ let the pyre burn you wept
Burn burn

                              Burn far beyond
This place this year into
A clearing where the blackened soul can stand
Green-leafed and rooted still

                              He took his life
Is quiet as breathing
It makes hardly any sound

                                        (1961)

A winter fable

Salzburg is like a crystal palace in the winter
Christmas eve the time to go there
With bells in ears even if the heart
Grieves an old woman quaking in a shawl
On Mozart's doorstep asking that his hand
Dispense his gold turn light upon the keys again
And still again illuminate those rooms in which the threads of music
Spindle revolve the stage-sets bright as
Separate fires kindled

There is another stage so hot in color
That the eyes cry curtain curtain curtain
But it will not fall
Act after act they mime their toothless roles
Without foyer or remission without program five
Or six old hags cast up against the wainscoting
Of Grand Central's ladies' room the shifting
Tide of others comes and goes using the lavabos
The central grandness of their lives discarding
Those without train-time or destination the hags
With legs as gnarled as Christmas stockings
Packed with varicose veins instead of presents
Their shoes split to allow their bunions
To take the air this place
That offers heat and light for nothing

Has become their salon the trains stammer
Accompaniment to their silent guffawing
Here they entertain the creaking dreams
Of youth malodorous by this time here
Pour tea from thermos bottles with the
Vacuum lining shattered like the moon on water
The tin casing decorated with safety pins
Necklaces of paper clips with pages
From the Bible torn in four and stapled
Tea laced with a shot of something else not very
Savory their invisible guests no more
Nor less than the inebriated wraiths of
—what? Try to say it without the mouth
Splitting the face with grinning from ear
To ear even the letters of the alphabet refuse
To spell it

> (I swear if I was a man I'd wait
> With orchids at that stage door with "Ladies"
> Written above the portal I'd take them home
> The lot of them establish them
> In solace these with the cumbersome shape
> Of mothers the three categories of mother
>   the neglected
>   the long forgotten
>   and the dead)

It was eleven o'clock on this particular Christmas eve when a neatly dressed Negro lady came in to the ladies' waiting room, pulling behind her a little wagon made out of a packing box and painted red. It had bright black wire-spoked wheels, this snappy little wagon, and a long flexible chromium shaft by which the lady, neat as a needle, guided it over the damp and odorous tiles. In the wagon, on a cushion, sat a cat with the head of a male ballet dancer. His coat was finer than satin, and his markings were such that he appeared to wear a dark hood drawn low upon his brow. At the sight of this cat in the wagon, the eyes of the five or six old hags returned from the vast Saharas of the past, from the wide reaches of catastrophe, and halted at this oasis, bitter as arsenic, the waters of it, if they only knew.

"Now, Leonard, you just take a look around and make up your mind," the Negro lady said. She had the look of a schoolteacher about her, perhaps because of the finicky statement of her dark blue outfit and the gold-rimmed spectacles she wore. Not even the lacy white wool scarf laid over her hair could take the edge of discipline away. She was made out of flat narrow laths, or so it seemed, so thin you would think she was starving to death, only nobody starves in New York City (not even the Bowery bum who died last week standing upright in a doorway. He didn't starve, he froze to death, the newspaper said, although the autopsy showed he hadn't eaten since several days).

"Leonard's a boy of discrimination. You know that, Mrs. Morgan," the Negro lady was saying to the ladies'-room attendant. "You know as well as I do that he'll always pick out the nicest-looking lady in the place, and I don't mean empty prettiness. He looks for character." The cat had an emerald leather collar around his licorice neck, and he was chained to the wagon by a nickel chain. He lowered his head like a cobra and peered at the ladies who came and went in front of the mirrors, running combs through their hair, shaking the cinders of Pittsburgh or Chicago, or the sands of Atlantic City, out of their locks, and putting something else quickly in its place so that nobody would know.

The hags were immobile as Christmas stockings spiked to the chimney piece, and the eyes of the chipper travelers were fixed on the swinging doors of the cabinays, hoping to slither their buxom forms in without benefit of dime dropped in the slot. One of these was so dressed that she looked like two bloated leopards stitched together. There she stood, buttoned short and broad and irate in her painted plush, elbowing her way through the accumulated others, upbraiding her own reflection in fury before she recognized it was herself before her, outraged with passion in the glass.

"I'm just letting you take your time, Leonard. You know that," the Negro lady said to the cat. They did not offer romance, friendship, or any of the popular commodities, but in the end they possessed the entire scene. She had now grown a stick (like Aaron's rod) from her right hand, and she tapped the cat on the shoulder with the tip of it. "Leonard, you're being very choosy tonight. Sometimes he makes up his mind in a minute," she said, and she flicked at him sharply with the cane. When she touched him thus, the satin skin of his shoulder jerked, and he peered with gold-eyed gravity at the women who had now begun to gather close. It was clear to all he was seeking something different from what he saw. Let me tell you that the stick was like a vein through which the power of the Negro lady's narrow will sought vainly to pass into the cat. "Sometimes he'll jump right down and start sloping around," she was saying as she whacked him with the stick again. "Leonard," she said, and her voice was rising, "you just pick out the lady who looks nicest to you, and you tell us what you think of her. We're all waiting on you, Leonard," she said.

"Rainy days she'll bring him in here and he'll have a yellow slicker on, and a rain hat tied under his chin," said the ladies'-room attendant. "He has a bunch of fortunes in that little bag on the seat. He chooses a lady, and she gives him a little something, and then she gets her fortune all printed out." "A little something?" cried the woman whose squat and terrible body the bloated leopards were constantly devouring. "Maybe a quarter," said the attendant. "Nobody can tell if he's going to pick out a young girl or a woman wise in the ways of love," said the Negro lady. "It's class he's interested in."

> Beyond the circle of women who pressed close
> The hags sat on the leather benches
> Sat against the wainscoting sat
> With their haunches quivering sat
> Their eyes opaque believing that
> Now with sleigh bells in the ears
> Frost on the lashes now with the arteries

Of Christmas hardening justice was about
To be meted out.

The old women were ready to take
Their uppers and lowers out of their
Handbags and clamp them in their jaws again
Were dying to frizz the strands
Of their lank hair between forefinger
And thumb to push their legs out of sight
Under the ruptured benches if only
He would look their way
If he had stretched one paw one claw
The toothpick or fishbone of a whisker in their
Direction they would have taken the
Withered masks from their faces and let
The tears of self-pity, gratitude (synonymous
With greed and lust) fall from
Their orbs.

"Oh, I know him well, the crafty puss!" said his mistress while the women watched. "He looks so frank and honest, doesn't he, with that topaz stare! I tell you he'll do this sometimes just to drive me to cut my throat! Leonard!" she cried out sharply, but he did not move. He sat, sleek and competent in his ballet dancer's black silk tights and his smooth imitation sealskin hood, wanting none of what he saw. "You jump right down now and go to the lady you think is the nicest here tonight. You go and do it, Leonard, and maybe she'll give you a quarter, or if you choose right, fifty cents. It's Christmas, Leonard!" But what did he do instead but turn on his cushion and lie down, drawing the glossy rope of his tail around his elbows, and narrowing his shoulders so that they need bear no responsibility.

"That's your decision, is it? Then no liver tomorrow, Leonard!" said the Negro lady, and her voice was tight and small. Suddenly she lifted the stick and struck the cat five cracking blows. It seemed his spine must break in two from the force of the stick, but it did not break, nor did he writhe like a half-killed cobra in the waiting-room dirt. Instead, he cringed in a corner of the wagon, flat as a cockroach, his eyes gone black with mourning for the dignity she had taken away. "So you aren't going to choose anyone tonight? So nobody's good enough for Leonard, is that it?" she shouted, and struck at his skull. But now he reared up on his hind legs and fought the cane, while the circle of women moved away.

> The water ran into the basins
> The toilets flushed and
> Mrs. Morgan picked up
> The dripping mop and pushed it
> Across the floor the hags
> Watched from the benches watched
> And took their thermos bottles out
> To offer drinks to wraiths that
> Twisted on the air they watched
> The Negro lady strike
> At the cat's quick subtle life
> Now become the bone and flesh of what
> They once had been neat-ankled silken-haired
> Their red gums grinning at the Negro lady
> As attrition and the cat the shackled will.

(1960)

A poem of gratitude

FOR CARESSE CROSBY

Now the tide is coming in, each long, low, hastening wave in the cove
Arching a little, barely spuming, but running
Into the salt grass the way a river whispers in.
I see the fluid fingers pass along the shallows
And the scalpel of the jetty probing, and you are far
In ether-sleep, the small door of your heart first swinging wide,
Then closing, opening and closing, hinged not by tissue, but by metal
In their quick, gloved hands. I think of you,
Tender as spring fern in the rain, pliant as seaweed
In man's current. I see the waves ride swiftly in
On the sands, see the weather vane reel on its pole,
Its fluctuating arrow crying: Here, here, there is breath!
And I say: This is good, it must be good, this omen. I have known
The meridian of your heart too long, too long,
To accept any break in it, any crack, any faltering.

Now the far star of the lighthouse shines,
And the moon floats in the trees, rosy and silken. The waves run softly
    in,
And the nighthawk gives its brief, fierce cry
As you once cried. Where you now lie, the tide of ether ebbs,

And the small door of your heart opens and closes, opens,
But now it is the south wind of your blood that fans it wide.

In the clear dusk, I put my arm around the memory of all we were,
Of all we were not, and I am happy,
Watching the cove hold in its curve the deepening waters of the tide.

(1958)

The new emigration

(On reading a French reporter's account of the clandestine crossings from Spain)

They cross the frontier as their names cross your pages,
Dark-eyed, slender-throated, with tongues that have run
As mercury runs to the fever of sun. But now as I read, as I write,
They are crossing by moon, traps shut, guitars muted,
Fox-smell on the night, without passport or visa or money to ring. So they
  come
Through the trees. They are young, but they wear
Bleak masks of hunger, coats tight in the armpits, too short in the sleeve.
But hope can be cloak, can be shoes on the feet, can be lash
Out of bull hide still tough in the dust when the trumpets are done.

The joke of it is they are not in the news. Not Koreans who follow
  torrent and stone
From northward to southward; not Germans who flux from east toward
  the west.
These quick-eyed, these young, who are musical-tongued, have blood
  that is lava
Pursuing the vein from lover to lover, Spaniard to Spaniard, dead man
  to son,
And no milestone to say it is here, the frontier.

But the dead of wars and hunger rattling in their beds
Are stilled in the brief, sweet moment that the thin-ribbed come
Out of the province of Zamora, out of Asturias, Seville,
Bearing in flight their country, bearing Spain,
Leaving the soft-voweled names behind to genuflection; not to
    bend
Elbow or knee again, but to cross before the altars of wild
    olive trees,
Upright, like men.
Here France is France, wide open in the dark,
Who takes them in.

Does history state that all men seek the classical
Grave face of liberty, leave interchangeable footprints as they run,
Communicate identical dreams from man to son,
Whatever the continent or century? Listen. Men
Are as different as their climates are. The pride of some
Lies in the passage of firearms from palm to palm,
War after war, along an iron Rhine; in some
The honeycomb has hardened like an artery. But not in these
Whose presence states a frontier is that undetermined place
One comes up alone at night, in life, and crosses
Even if afraid.

(*1956*)

World tour

FOR MY DAUGHTER, SHARON

Take determination, take it apart; stamp out the music from its means,
Meet the violently fixed eyes of its enacted ends, split
Not the origins but the performances of war and peace and in
Their sundered dramas watch the actors fail, fumble their lines,
The curtain quiver to rise and then expire; take gray-leafed mimosa,
Palm, marigold, planted as regular as prison stripes along the new
Italian roads laid to conduct the world's tour of the curious and idle
      through
Poverty; take them and break their stems for sap, and as they wither
      hear
It whispered: "We are committed not to fade whatever the season;
Like iron vegetation, neither to wilt or shed petal so no eye reads
Between our leaves the lices' determination in children's hair, the
Scleritis flung into their eyes like red hot sand." This open air
You take within your substance then expel, isolates the open, jaunty,
      tragic,
Lordly, free; tainted by method, pock-marked with spit, employed by
      Franco in soliciting
Tourists this summer to come visit, relax in; see the trapped speechless
      air
Of Negroes and the mob already at the door, or that the old and nameless
Jews, scientists or tradesmen too obscure for ransom wear. Take ransom,
Take it: a frantic accumulation of grief, protest, and fury paid
Year after gullible year before the mutilated corpse of youth is found,

Rain-sodden, its betrayed mouth set, dead at the very moment
The currency was passed and rotting in the underbrush of home.

    (You know, I had the funniest dream last night,
    She said when she came home from school.
    I was standing in the chapel just like every day
    And all the other kids were there, of course,
    And then this man, you know, a kind of short thin man,
    Came in and took the middle of the floor
    As if he was going to make a speech or something.
    But before he got a word out, I don't know how it was,
    The whole top of his head started to burn.
    Oh, I forgot to say that all the time
    He had his hand up in, you know, like the fascist salute
    And his other hand was held up shaking in a clenched fist all
        the time.
    Well, after his head caught on fire, he kept on burning,
    His hair, and face, and neck, and everything straight down
    And nobody did anything or said a word. It was cuckoo.
    But just before his shoes burned he said: "Vive
    La Patrie!" I don't know what said it, I mean,
    Whether it was his shoes said it or what, but
    Anyway he said: "Vive la Patrie!" with a funny accent
    Like a foreigner trying to speak French, and in my dream
    I did the dumbest thing. I fell down on my knees
    In front of all the other kids and started praying).

Come here, come in with me and let follow
Those faces which pursue you:
The sick, wild, reticent, at bay,
Who do not crowd but quietly heel
And do not want but take the glass to drink
And cannot, but let spill, let fall,
Let dribble down their chins, let go
Pride's remnants, massacred but quick still,
Clotted, jugulated veins, conduits

In bleeding fragments, valves to gasp
Flapping from the air's white strangling net
Down shirt front to floor and there not stop
Their dying. Come in and say it. Let
The gaunt musicians begin, let the outcast, the hungry, condemned,
Tied ankle to ankle and coupled,
Jerk the marathon dance, stumble drunk
To the music, but sober, swoop low to the boards
At the last, but change partners and hands for the lynching.

(1938)

A communication to Nancy Cunard

These are not words set down for the rejected
Nor for outcasts cast by the mind's pity
Beyond the aid of lip or hand or from the speech
Of fires lighted in the wilderness by lost men
Reaching in fright and passion to each other.
This is not for the abandoned to hear.

It begins in the dark on a boxcar floor, the groaning timber
Stretched from bolt to bolt above the freight-train wheels
That grind and cry aloud like hounds upon the trail, the breathing
    weaving
Unseen within the dark from mouth to nostril, nostril to speaking mouth.
This is the theme of it, stated by one girl in a boxcar saying:
"Christ, what they pay you don't keep body and soul together."
"Where was you working?" "Working in a mill town."
The other girl in the corner saying: "Working the men when we could
    get them."
"Christ, what they pay you," wove the sound of breathing, "don't keep
    shoes on your feet.
Don't feed you. That's why we're shoving on."

(This is not for Virginia Price or Ruby Bates, the white girls dressed like
boys to go; not for Ozie Powell, six years in a cell playing the little harp
he played tap-dancing on the boxcar boards; not for Olen Montgomery,
the blind boy traveling towards Memphis that night, hopping a ride to

find a doctor who could cure his eyes; not for Eugene Williams or
Charlie Weems, not for Willie Robertson nor for Leroy and Andy
Wright, thirteen years old the time in March they took him off the train
in Paint Rock, Alabama; this is not for Clarence Norris or Haywood
Patterson, sentenced three times to die.)

> This is for the sheriff with a gold lodge pin
> And for the jury venireman who said: "Now, mos' folk don't
>   go on
> And think things out. The Bible never speaks
> Of sexual intercourses. It jus' says a man knows a woman.
> So after Cain killed Abel he went off and knew a woman
> In the land of Nod. But the Bible tells as how
> There couldn't be no human folk there then.
> Now, jus' put two and two together. Cain had offspring
> In the land of Nod so he musta had him a female baboon
> Or chimpanzee or somethin' like it.
> And that's how the nigger race begun."

This is for the Sunday-school teacher with the tobacco plug
Who addressed the jury, the juice splattering on the wall,
Pleading: "Whether in overalls or furs a woman is protected by the
    Alabama law
Against the vilest crime the human species knows. Now, even dogs choose
    their mates,
But these nine boys are lower than the birds of the air,
Lower than the fish in the sea, lower than the beasts of the fields.
There is a law reaching down from the mountaintops to the swamps and
    caves—
It's the wisdom of the ages, there to protect the sacred parts of the female
    species
Without them having to buckle around their middles
Six-shooters or some other method of defense."

> This is set down for the others: people who go and come,
> Open a door and pass through it, walk in the streets

With the shops lit, loitering, lingering, gazing.
This is for two men riding, Deputy Sheriff Sandlin, Deputy
    Sheriff Blacock,
With Ozie Powell, handcuffed. Twelve miles out of Cullman
They shot him through the head.

THE TESTIMONY

Haywood Patterson:	*Victoria Price*
"So here goes an I shell try	
Faitfully an I possibly can	
Reference to myself in	"I
particularly	cain't
And concerning the other boys	remember."
personal pride	
And life time up to now.	
You must be patiene with me	
and remember	
Most of my English is not of	"I
much interest	cain't
And that I am continually	remember."
Stopping and searching for the	
word."	

So here goes and I shall try faithfully as possible to tell you as I understand if not mistaken that Olen Montgomery, who was part blind then, kept saying because of the dark there was inside the boxcar and outside it: "It sure don't seem to me we're getting anywheres. It sure don't seem like it to me." I and my three comrades whom were with me, namely Roy Wright and his brother Andy and Eugene Williams, and about my character I have always been a good natural sort of boy, but as far as I am personally concerned about those pictures of me in the papers, why they are more or less undoubtedly not having the full likeness of me for I am a sight better-looking than those pictures make me out. Why all my life I spent in and around working for Jews in their stores and so on and I have quite a few Jew friends whom can and always have gave me a good reputation as having regards for those whom have regards for me. The depression ran me away from home, I was off on my way to try my very best to find some work some elsewhere but misfortune befalled me without a moving cause. For it is events and misfortune which happens to people and how some must whom are less fortunate have their lives taken from them and how people die in chair for what they do not do.

THE SPIRITUAL FOR NINE VOICES

I went last night to a turkey feast (Oh, God, don't fail your children
    now!)
My people were sitting there the way they'll sit in heaven
With their wings spread out and their hearts all singing
Their mouths full of food and the table set with glass
(Oh, God, don't fail your children now!)
There were poor men sitting with their fingers dripping honey
All the ugly sisters were fair. I saw my brother who never had a
    penny
With a silk shirt on and a pair of golden braces
And gems strewn through his hair.

(Were you looking, Father, when the sheriffs came in?
Was your face turned towards us when they had their say?)

    There was baked sweet potato and fried corn pone
    There was eating galore, there was plenty in the horn.
(Were you there when Victoria Price took the stand?
Did you see the state attorney with her drawers in his hand?
Did you hear him asking for me to burn?)

    There were oysters cooked in amplitude
    There was sauce in every mouth.
    There was ham done slow in spice and clove

And chicken enough for the young and the old.
(Was it you stilled the water on horse-swapping day
When the mob came to the jail? Was it you come out in a long
    tail coat
Come dancing high with the word in your mouth?)

I saw my sister who never had a cent
Come shaking and shuffling between the seats.
Her hair was straight and her nails were pointed
Her breasts were high and her legs double-jointed.

(Oh, God, don't fail your children now!)

THE SENTENCE

Hear how it goes, the wheels of it traveling fast on the rails
    The boxcars, the gondolas running drunk through the night.
Hear the long high wail as it flashes through stations unlit
    Past signals ungiven, running wild through a country
A time when sleepers rouse in their beds and listen
    And cannot sleep again.
Hear it passing in no direction, to no destination
Carrying people caught in the boxcars, trapped on the coupled chert cars
(Hear the rattle of gravel as it rides whistling through the day and night.)
Not the old or the young on it, nor people with any difference in their
    color or shape,
Not girls or men, Negroes or white, but people with this in common:
People that no one had use for, had nothing to give to, no place to offer
But the cars of a freight train careening through Paint Rock, through
    Memphis,
    Through town after town without halting.
    The loose hands hang down, and swing with the swing of the train
        in the darkness,
    Holding nothing but poverty, syphilis white as a handful of dust,
        taking nothing as baggage

But the sound of the harp Ozie Powell is playing or the voice of
   Montgomery
Half-blind in oblivion saying: "It sure don't seem to me like we're
   getting anywheres.
It don't seem to me like we're getting anywheres at all."

(1937)

A glad day for Laurence Vail

This year you gave me
The black flanks of a mule
To ripple and strain under me
And one day after another yellow as cantaloupe
Hung over my saddle like a melon-flower

The day was dark when we set out over and time was spent on face of
flower too bright for ordinary weather bred to applause of bolt or thunder
its petals riveted flake by flake in blue but richer. Here people and stock
and vegetation breathed air not rarer but laid the nostril wide like
silver rings set one upon another in. Dark was the day the flock came
close for comfort asking sirup to soothe devouring shears to travel through
their fleece.

But it was a glad day came after
The sun was born with a cape of fire
Came jigging stamping clapping in
It was a glad day came after

The speech that suits my ear and mouth is talk of cloth or keys or
bread. A man's mind should be elsewhere. By climbing higher he pursues
the sun where taste and scent and common shape have petrified have
turned to glass. Quiet and pure her eye is shaped to gather landmarks
herbs and flowers and mineral fists no light to set against the black
advance. (But a long time I shall see the stony-footed chamois they

brought in at night in a leather coat on a mule's back, like a man they had murdered, lifting him out by the chin and gazing into eyes as brown as deep as limpid death.)

But a glad day came after
The sun was born with a girdle of fire
Came stamping jigging clapping in
With his hands in his pockets and his pockets in his pants
It was a glad day came after

There is another season that comes after spring, not summer but a month who combs her hair, and braids it fast with winds and lingers late, and will not heed the elements' complaint. There is a season strips the mountains bare of twig or blade and straps with violent paths the wilderness that quivers like a carp. And rocks are stern in language and in grace as words said of them or as dance upon. Nor move not heedlessly from place to place like facile-footed men but bide their time.

There is another season after spring when lights as white as fountains spray the north, and leaves like tar drip thickly from the bough and cast a cloak of elegance around. When odor leaps full-blown upon the stalk and music runs in hard steep flights of sound, when taste lies slow as honey in the mouth and drifts of snow lie changeless at the pass.

It was a glad day came after

Allos, when the mules come up out of the valley their old knees knuckle the skyline. There is no grip for the beasts' feet or food for their loose lips hanging other than thistles churned to fresh cream in their jaws, other than weather to flow whether to floe or mountain lake held fast. Allos, the times of year lie in the sireling of ewelings, in the bearing of a lamb in early darkness. Allos, under the armor which a breath might pierce, the water holds bouquets of trout and cresses. We went up to follow the spring's coming and the hard chatter of snows gone thin for water falling forever out of the mouth of sound.

It was a glad day came after
The sun was born with a hand of fire
You took me so high that the beasts faltered in sweat
We followed until twilight
The tongues of the sheep-bells calling
And your feet seeking root in the shale ahead.

(1930)

A comeallye for
Robert Carlton Brown

I

There was one man and he was not an Irishman but he might have been one with all his lying thieving ways. Nor was he a priest but he might have been one because of his way of walking through the woods as if it were a church, murmuring, with a cross around his neck that he kept there for the shape of the thing. Gothic or Corinthian the pillars or the pine trees might have been for all he knew the difference. But if a beast were sick he could turn up its hoofs and nurse it like a mother.

> George, and will ye be my bridegroom

was the refrain in the wind and in the mosses whose species he knew in the sole of his foot. He was busy following the soft secret track of a deer running and he could not very well reply.

> And will ye be my bridegroom
> And wear a crown of glory

In stomping your foot in that impatient way, he said, you stomped ou the mark of the deer or whatever it was running.

When he rolled back the sleeves of his shirt there were his arms o bare like twists of taffy. One of them he put lovingly around the s bowed neck of the ailing cow. The lady had lost her cud, it had dropp into one of her stomachs. A cud, he said, it is made of daisy hearts ;

73

dandelions. He held a bouquet of it flowering in his hand. Her rosy tongue hung through her teeth, her noble breath lolled on this couch of flesh, her cloven feet gave battle to a thousand blades of grass.

> And will you be my bridegroom, George,
> And wear a crown of glory
> Will you take the dark for an evening cloak
> And the Pleiades for planets
> Will you dance on the turnpike with me, George

And will you shut up for a half a minute, said George, until I get this cud in her mouth can't you be quiet?

He took care of the stock. He was a horse thief and a liar, it turned out. He was no good to anybody at all. Hours he wasted in making necklaces for the goats to wear to market. His fingers were as thick as dice, and just as square as. Do you think men lie still when they're dead, I said to him. Do you think men who could harpoon a whale, tan a lion, geld a stallion would ever take it lying down? I bet they stand up shouting, do you bet they're quiet? Can't you be quiet yourself, said George, until I've found one with four leaves to it?

II

When the old women went into church it was for a sight of the Bridegroom. They came along the roads and peering into the ditches, keeping their eyes and their ears cocked for a sign of him, for he was on the run. At high mass a special service was sung for him. It soared from the young boys' throats, rose high and clear against the stone and the remains of it dropped down the spine like icy drops of water.

> He is fairer than May weather and the fruit trees, they sang.
> Happy is the woman to whom he gives his hand.
> (When he lifts up his eyes, the rivers leap with salmon.
> He need only whistle for the waves to sound his name.)

I have seen him cross the lake like a rainbow crossing.
In summer he runs like a comb through the rye.
Often have I hung my head for shame when he passed me.
His gait is swift, his flesh is tough as leather.
His heart is like a hawk's flight.

Ah-ah-ah-men!

From the altars and the chapels had the Bridegroom departed. The crosses all over the land were as empty as the loins of the Virgin. Nothing of any value had he left behind. The gold was gone from the vestry and the velvet from the wardrobe. He had stripped the braid from the bishops' dresses and cut the lace from the abbots' gowns. Somewhere, it might very well be in the bogs, he was melting down the gold of the loving cup and the silver of the tabernacle maybe.

In the church did the voices of the choirboys exhort him, but he had no time for it. He had a hand like a kick in the tail. Some of them had felt the side of it on their bottoms, not once but many's the time. No matter how loud they sung, it would do them no good now. The Bridegroom had staunched his wounds, girded up his loins, and silently gone thence.

III

THE SONG OF THE BRIDEGROOM

I've been crying in the dark for my own land
You can know it by the way its rivers flow
Like a blindman I could find my way betwixt them
From the queer coast to the rocky jaws of Ulster
(By running my fingers over their faces would I tell them,
The northmen or the south, by the way their hearts were beating.)

I've been crying like a child for my own land
Or like a man bereaved. Let drink cascade

From mouth to heart, fall cupped in kneecap,
Cavort to temple, turn tongue to fire and breast to pulpit.
I shall die alone
Without the bride's soft arms repining
The ringdove sobbing, the marrow melting.
(By the way their color changes when I strike them drunk
Can I weed out the men of North Ireland from those of the South
And God deliver me.) Let whiskey sing requiem for us:
Ah, what is it they have in their eye that nobody else has
In the curse, the kiss, the hot look on the face
That nobody else has. Whisper what is it or was it
That nobody else has and what will it ever be?

(1930)

76

A valentine for Harry Crosby

I offer you a heart of red isinglass outlined in tinsel.
If you hold it to the light you can see the sun shining through.
It is as beautiful as a goat's eye lit with anger,
It is as grave as the pines that have grown taller and taller
Lingering along the road.

Now is the year as lacy as a gown
That on the staircase runs a step or two behind
Laced with fine frost and hung with falling snow,
Soft to the ankles as a swollen stream that follows and booms down the
    shallow bed
That heels in fleeing past have spaded out; those small half moons of
    tender heels
Which rose and waned like planets in your heavens,
Young coral-nostrilled heels wading the creeks that now have broken
    through
To sniff and bleat and nibble at the edge of spring.

THE COMPLAINT IN IT

Turn back your hair in a pompadour for the days
That have gone dwindling, that have tapered,
That have burned down to the very end;

77

For the days when my grandmother's hair was arrowlace
Of fern glossed red by the frost;
For the days spread like a goose's wing,
Forgotten in swivel chairs in Washington, forgotten,
In the Government Offices with a wig on, forgotten,
Forgotten, the apples rotting in the orchard,
The year left nailed in warning like a dead hawk on the barn door.

He is to be read of in history,
A gentle gentleman speaking words that shake the teeth in the head.
When the insomnia had him by the eyelids
He left his bed and walked out on the sea.
The quick little fish with their deep mouths remember
How his feet walked out on the brine of the waves.
There it is written in the cold hearts of them
In the cold tart blood that lies still on their bones,
How Jesus left his bed and Jesus left his women
And finely and shapely walked the salt of the sea.
The end of the tale is of Jesus like a butterfly
With his arms pinned open and his legs braided up with pain.

THE REFRAIN

I would give you a day to go naked in.
Not this one, for it fits you badly,
And the blades of winter curved to your jaw's pumice
Whittle you to the bone.
　　Other days more to your measure:
June days that pinched your weeping armpits, hugged the tight drums
Of your knees, clasped the shin drumsticks that rattled on them;
Checked April first days or double-breasted Christmases
Buttoned from gullet to ankle. But February's! with this one set in the
　　middle
Like a bonfire at which to thaw your fingers.

Now is the year as lacy as a gown
Which curious winds blow up and down at will.
Hollowed for sound upon the heathen fields
The crocus quivers like a young goat's ear.
And you, what month are you, what wind that lies
As sweet as squirrel skin underneath the chin?
What time of year that sows no seeds, nor reaps none,
Gives the weeded ground, the barren branch, makes way for spring
By root, by sap; draws close the February rains and bids them snuff
    the beacon of your life
And let you sleep and sleep with sleep and sleep awhile
Until a fresher season swoons between your thighs.

(1929)

Dedicated to Robert McAlmon

What good did your blood do you
if it gave you honey under the tongue
a deep valley for the wind to lie still in
and sent you wandering
over the dams of timber sawn white by the teeth of beavers
over the badger country for hawthorn sap
and the sight of wild onion

It would be a good thing to sit quiet
Flesh salted on the wharves and eyes clean with brine
Talking chewing and talking
To sit with the bricks swept
and the wind steady as light shafting seaward
and the hard foam clanging upon the land

It would be a good thing to return
out of the cold now the seams in the ice cracking wide
the wild heart whoring the hard eye warming
to the nest of an oriole hanging like iron grapes in a pine
Talk about the afternoon you found a young goat
and brought it home in your arms with its legs dangling
and its muzzle pressed cool and wet on your face
Eyes beckoning a sail off the cold plains that lie like priests' gowns
    discarded

80

and the priests themselves in their white skins
lost in the music of the waves

What good did it do you
the softness of gulls' breasts in you
and a winter as hard as any winter
that lies in an old man's heart
Buried deep so that no light of the moon
or any light can draw you
out of the corpse-soil and the quiet
out of the nights that cry like wolves in the dark

(1928)

The only bird that sang

The church mice had been bombed out of Albert
The corporal under the gas ring
Said he would get out for good this time
If the roquefort didn't sit still on the plate
Instead of bruising its bottom green on the table.
For the French it was the way it ought to be
The roquefort but the corporal had a sore throat
And it had been raining all day

    They have planted a flower
    Under the rose trees at Albert
    Pneumonia cool as edelweiss
    Was the last thing blooming into a song for him
    Singing to him like a mama
    This century the war that came whistling
    The only bird that sang

After forty-eight hours of marriage with the elements
The corporal took out the roquefort
He had brought with him for company
It was winging in his pocket like a hummingbird
In Amiens he felt it out saying soit sage to it
In Albert he saw the gangrene on it was eating closer
And closer to the bone

Spring came
Without pulpit flowers
Or boiling tubs of sassafras
A long time
Since spring had come in a new way
The cannons bucked like goats
Along the edge of it
The veins broke wide and flowered
The corporal at Albert
Fell into decay

In response to the bird's clarion
There came the highest qualities of gentlemen
The girls (all ladies) nursing their way through it
The towns were proud the trains the sky the liners
Staterooms wharves the skyline proud
The army proud to wear them strong as hyacinths
The surgeons happy and proud
The wings of airplanes and proud the sheets
The pillows bedpans congressmen the subways proud
The president the frigidaire turned proud
We are proud of our girls who are over there.

Oh, Leda, how did the swan fly in hospitals
How from the rushes did its wings lift
The iron mirror of the lake
Churned to a wheel from indolence to anger
The small black budding spring
Pressed close between the breasts

The corporal died happy to have had
A flower nourished by his nine red yards
Of clogged intestines planted where he fell
Others were put seven hundred at a time
Under a truckload of small rock and gravel
In the way that any group

Could be disposed of without a loss to history
Beyond beauty of line squandered and wiped out
Tied still beneath gray wire wreaths with
Written in celluloid
Petits anges au ciel volez volez pour nous

    I remember them
    With Christmas trees
    With lollypops
    Eating their soup quietly
    Out of the sides of their spoons
    They made life a meal of
    Young chop suey fresh roots and tendrils
    Of peaches burning
    And of lemon ice

The corporal died knowing that if Debs
Had been president there'd be a german general
In every maiden lady's bed
Contented to masturbate the lady mules
In spare time
Talking of war not as it was to him
A burden which in honor he could not put down

    There will be more sons
    More husbands fathers
    To breed for another springtime
    To stamp for another season for hallelujah
    Not the pruning and the sobbing of ringdoves
    In the willows soft with repining
    Now we are stricken with peace
        We are stricken with peace
            We are stricken

                  (1928)

A letter to Francis Picabia

I

There is one country
　　and no shame to it
For having a heart hot in the bosom
Or songs in the mouth humming
That servant-girls sing at their dishes
Wherever the men of it are
Are the laughter and the sorrowing
　　of their own land
And whenever a stranger speaks
It is an odd word he is saying

The rich coins sing in the hands of them
But whether it is I am deaf now
Or whether it is I am blinded
By the thought of the dead
　　rank in my eyes even
I am weary
　　for speech like new cress in the river
I am sick for a sight of him
　　for whom my tears fall

II

I ask more of this season
Than leaves seeking the ground
    birds guiding the wind south
    or a doorstep swept clean for winter
No lost things
    fingers of stars pointing out
    steps on the wet grass
    the moon ringing the hay-bells the frogs crying
    out upon what a mouth said or remembered

Or the eyelids of one town lifting
    No answer
From fields struck dumb with frost
But a new season blooming
    a new history of feast-days
For a young man who died one autumn

III

If I thought
    this is the way I'd be
Waiting if the door
    let him in
    lock of hair blown on the room's face
I'd be combing it
    back of my ears if I
Thought he'd be growing up in the glass
This is the way my legs
    crossed and my hands
        lying

If I thought I could
      see him make sugars fly
up his cuffs after dinner find
      potatoes hot in the dogs' ears
if I thought I could
      hear the thin bark of
his shoes on the gravel this is the way
      my eyes waiting
and my heart crying until
      I be dead with him

(*1927*)

In defense of homosexuality

I speak of it as a thing with a future
At present badly done by amateurs neglecting
The opportunity to be discriminating

It being an occupation in itself
It should not be confused with reticence
Or the perceptions of a shy man
Nor should it be segregated on a question of morality

To fit the part the incentive
Must be more than casual
Rather a weakness at the very roots
An appetite which leaves one flat, an inability
To get into the dirt, thread worms upon a hook,
Wash a floor clean; a vacancy
Which cannot read a page without a recognition
Of the symmetry of the thumb lying along it;
A similarity of gesture as professional as the whore's
And to the tough taste as flavorless
The loyalties of such are more perishable
Than the crust of an egg

A dislike of sweat and odor, of blowing the nose,
Of raising children clears the emotions to the hem of the garment only.

(O how sacred is the hem of thy garment hem of thy eyelid hem
    of thy hem
O how sacred art thou to me thou delicate-veined thou wild boy.
Benvenuto swathed in silks the limbs of his fresh one his virgin
And the boy went among the women as a girl and made free with them
And then told them that he was with child
And the women did lay their compassionate hands upon his belly
And upon his limbs and upon the flesh of his thighs
In commiseration, and then were their hearts rended with sweet anguish
And with terror as the rod blossomed in their fingers.)

By incentive is meant that fidelity to purpose
Which determines one to hold a parasol
Over tomato plants to shield them from the elements.
I prefer a rabbit neatly killed (to serve a purpose not create one)
Who under the knife blade peels like a ripe fig
The skin while still warm ripped in a piece from the royal satin flesh
Which it has lipped with intimate tenacity
Such a caress is worth a generation of these indecisions
We are asked to accept as celebration of a genuine passion

Nor does this signify that man cannot be to man a complement
Rather than a reflection of his own devices
Or that one might surprise those generosities, not of the mind
But richer, warmer than, which women find it imperative
(But no less valid) to make use of.
Nor does this state an apprehension placing
Women as women, men as fairies with a finality
That permits no accident

A cat is initiated by his mother's lovers under the lilac trees
A necessary preamble to the method and satisfaction of fathering kittens.
The human proceeds in the reverse direction
Establishing a home, hearth, fireside within those organs
Which respond like blind men to a lick of fire.

Put under glass some of them could be worn as cameos
Their femininity plumbed to the depths of
A tedious vocation as engrossing as bee-raising
And as monotonous to the outsider.

(1925)